GW01066318

ABOUT
THE AUTHOR

Simon Woodhead is Founder & CEO of Simwood. He is passionately committed to solving real-world problems with technology, and ensuring that technology and knowledge is freely available to those who need it. Simon is regularly asked to speak at technical conferences worldwide and what has been described as his 'irreverent swagger' is followed across the industry.

Simon has been engaged with technology and commerce since a very early age. His first career was in finance as a private client and gross fund manager. He was the youngest qualified member of the (now) Chartered Institute for Securities and Investment, and remains a Fellow. Simon was managing approximately £40 million by the age of 21. Along the way, he was repeatedly seconded to solve significant commercial and technical problems in the banks he worked for.

In 2016 he was elected a non-executive Director of the London Internet Exchange (LINX) - the world's largest mutual Internet Exchange, with over 20 terabits per second of capacity and 770 member ISPs from 76 different countries.

An Englishman who has made a Welsh mountain his home, Mountain Rescue was his outlet for 15 years. Now a father of three young girls with far less spare time, his recreation tends to involve chainsaws and helicopters.

Simwood eSMS Limited
Simwood House
Cube M4 Business Park
Old Gloucester Road
BRISTOL
BS16 1FX
United Kingdom

0330 122 3000

www.simwood.com

SPEAKING UP ON TELEPHONY RISKS

By Simon Woodhead

Foreword by Colonel John Doody

PLEASE TREAT THIS INFORMATION WITH THE CAUTION IT DESERVES

CONTENTS

FOREWORD

by Colonel (Retd) John Doody

Colonel John Doody was employed as Senior Military Officer and Head of Information Assurance Customer Services within the UK Government Communications Headquarters (GCHQ). With over 60 years' experience in the field of security, he is now the Director of Interlocutor Services – providing strategic information assurance and cryptographic advice to large enterprises. A distinguished lecturer and chair of discussions at leading security events, he was elevated to the Infosecurity Europe Hall of Fame in 2012.

"The challenge for us all is to reduce the cost of protection and increase the cost of attack."

I n my 60 years in the fields of Communications, Intelligence, and Cybersecurity, I have witnessed enormous change in telephony. Yet, in this time I have experienced no change in the desire of adversaries to steal information. At first hand, I have seen how today's threats to telephony networks, come from state exploitation, cyber criminals and hackers. At the state level, it is about gathering information on commercially sensitive intellectual property (IP), national economic information or strategic intelligence. Cyber criminals attack for money, while malicious hackers often just want to cause inconvenience to telephony users.

These challenges are no different to when I first started my career 60 years ago. However, what has changed is the technology, the amount of bandwidth and the much greater speeds that consumers rely on to communicate from anywhere, at any time, with anyone. These demand ever more complex telephony solutions, which in turn introduce vulnerabilities due to the sheer scale of the software programmes involved.

Having chaired discussions on the subject of security, one thing that organisations, large or small, desire are ways to combat the threats. For anyone concerned by telephony risks to business operations, this is a must-read guide. It presents valuable insights and guidance for those tasked with operating their networks safely by exploring pragmatic solutions to protect the company and its staff.

It is notable that many of the compromises made today are by people and not technology. Therefore, it is vital that Directors, CIOs and CTOs develop good policies, governance and practices that all staff can follow to be compliant. The challenge for all is to reduce the cost of PROTECTION and increase the cost of ATTACK, making an attacker's job much more difficult.

This guide provides sound advice that will help you minimise the risk to your business, reduce lost income and secure your intellectual property. I cannot recommend it highly enough.

INTRODUCTION

....

by Simon Woodhead
Founder and CEO of Simwood

When I started Simwood in 1996, it was based upon a belief that mobile phones and the Internet would individually gain popularity and stood strong potential to converge. That has certainly transpired but I did not anticipate the extent to which these tools, and the wider telecoms networks, would also be deployed as weapons.

In 2018, telecommunications networks are critical to business operations. Yet those same networks also present significant threat vectors. Most security vendors focus on IP networks and threats that can originate inside or outside a business over IP. At Simwood our attention has been drawn to the specific exploitation of telephony. That is because these are the networks that we participate in and understand for our core business.

In this guide, you will read about threats to your business that, in some cases, you may already have heard about. We expect, though, that you will also read about threats that are new to you. Your friendly telephone engineer may tell you these are impossible. Your telephone company will likely deny they exist. But they are possible and they do exist. We can say that because through our daily work we have to tackle them by empowering customers under threat on a global scale. Some examples may alarm you. You may even recall how some made high profile headlines and we'll signpost some of those throughout.

Whether or not these individual threats pose a risk to your business depends on how you are using the various telecommunications technologies available. However, it is our belief that knowledge is power. By sharing what we know about these threats we aim to help you identify any potential risks and deal with them in the future.

At Simwood, our business is about providing access to telecommunications networks to those who are able to consume it. Historically speaking, "able" has meant wholesale participants – for example, other telephone companies. However, with advancing technology the very definition of a "telephone company" has itself changed. It is now possible, and indeed common, for a telephone company to be a start-up or a one person, one bedroom operation. This democratisation of the market has been enabled by technology. Yet increased access, combined with increasing dependency in a world where knowledge is more widely shared, poses a great risk too.

"You will also read about threats that are new to you. Your friendly telephone engineer may tell you these are impossible. Your telephone company will likely deny they exist. But they are possible and they do exist"

Our business nowadays sees us increasingly servicing what we call 'post-service-provider enterprises'. These are often large corporates outside the telecommunication space but that have sufficient in-house resource to be considered a telephone company. We also find ourselves working in what you might call the intelligence space; using our significant technical expertise and infrastructure to prevent or mitigate the threats you will read about in this document.

In some cases, we are considered world experts and VoIP fraud is one such example. Our research is sought out by the world's largest telecommunications companies within hours of publication. In other areas, solutions are a work in progress or unavailable at present.

Simwood is a business built on transparency. It would be very easy for a document like this to come across as a brochure and we have tried to avoid that. I will say that working with us can overcome many of the issues where solutions do exist. For the purposes of this document, however, I have aimed to concentrate on the threats, the effects and the key considerations for your business.

Chapter 1

VoIP FRAUD

In 2011, we installed a number of generic 'honeypots' on our IP network. These were servers deployed across a moderately large block of unused IP addresses, and their sole purpose in life was to be attacked. We analysed the traffic these honeypots saw and published our findings.

One significant point of interest for us was that broadly 2% of the traffic reaching these hosts was SIP. SIP, or Session Initiation Protocol, is the primary protocol used for Voice over IP (VoIP) and is the primary service we sell. Our customers consume SIP services from us and generally sell SIP services to their customers. Therefore, this finding was of particular interest.

"The reality is that if you use VoIP within your organisation, you are a target"

So we then set about deploying SIP-specific honeypots across our network. These were commodity PBXs rather like our customers and your business might install.

Again, their sole purpose in life was to be hacked. When they were hacked we were able to analyse the patterns and the behaviour and we began publishing our findings as a series of data files available to the industry. In 2013 we published the very first edition of our "VoIP Fraud Analysis" document and began a series of presentations to educate the industry on the risks. We repeated this exercise in early 2016 by which time the document had gained significant awareness and its findings were eagerly anticipated by the largest players in the industry.

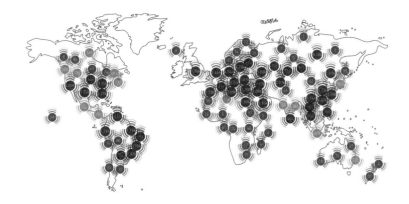

We will not repeat the contents of that document here, but it is available for any reader on request[1]. The main point to note here is that VoIP fraud has become significant business and is effectively a cash machine for organised crime and failed states.

The reality is that if you use VoIP within your organisation, you are a target. Your equipment is being scanned almost continuously. To prove this point in a previous presentation, we installed a new PBX on a commodity cloud provider's network. This was done largely to disprove the suggestion that Simwood saw a higher level of intrusion attempts across our own network because SIP was known to be our core business. While there may be some merits to this argument in terms of targeted attacks, we know that the majority of VoIP fraud incidents start with routine and widespread harvesting. That harvesting takes place across the Internet and across all Internet-connected devices, continuously. In our demonstration our newly installed PBX, away from our network, saw its first scan for SIP services within just 40 minutes. It proceeded through the various levels of subsequent attack escalation to a successful intrusion within 18 hours.

Had this been an actual PBX installed on a customer's premises, it is highly likely that the attacker would have gone on to send substantial volumes of expensive call traffic. Following a confirmed intrusion, a hacker will dial revenue generating numbers that are generally, but not always, in international destinations. They will continue to dial these numbers until they are stopped.

The duration of this revenue collection depends entirely on the speed and agility of the response by the victim or the victim's service provider. Simwood has made it our business to protect our customers, and in turn their customers, from voice fraud. We take a proactive stance. The majority of other providers sadly do not. We aim to identify these attacks and associated bad traffic in real time - before incurring large costs and sometimes before the visible attack starts at all - through

"VoIP fraud has become significant business and is effectively a cash machine for organised crime and failed states"

our monitoring and predictive technologies. By contrast, less agile providers link alerts into their billing in order to tell customers when they have reached a predetermined level of spend – i.e. the expense has already been incurred at a loss for the victim and a profit for the provider. Worse still, some simply operate end of the month billing, by which time several hundred thousand pounds of expensive calls could have been made. We would far sooner customers do not spend the money in the first place and that the VoIP fraud intrusion is entirely unsuccessful because it has been thwarted at its early stages. This has been one of our unique selling points for the last several years.

If you operate IP telephony in any form, not just SIP, you are at risk from this threat. There are, however, some basic and simple steps that you can take to protect yourself and these are outlined in our VoIP Fraud Analysis document. Most attacks are incredibly simple in their nature and origin, and thus easily mitigated. However, as easy victims become scarce the attacks will evolve. In fact, we are already seeing some incredibly sophisticated attacks, with patient and devious behaviour behind them. Long gone are the days when an attack was obvious from its sheer brute force and impatience. Nowadays, the attackers are patient, recognise the need to be discreet and they do significant homework into their victims' infrastructure before launching a substantial attack. Whilst it is relatively straightforward to protect your business, or to work with a competent, well-intentioned service provider that can, the cost of this attack vector should not be underestimated. Nor should the frequency of such attacks. In our experience, attacks are hardly ever publicised or disclosed to authorities. They will run into the region of thousands of pounds per hour and will run as long and as hard as the victim allows them to.

Enterprises with IP PBXs can make use of Simwood's highly available call termination services. We employ over 200 checks per call and in real-time to apply the intelligence learned from our honeypots and your specific settings. Settings can be applied per account or per individual 'trunk' (where a trunk could be a remote office or even a nomadic user). If you want to ensure your site in Leeds can not call outside the UK and the Manchester office can only call international destinations three times per day, we can do that. We will actively block calls and give you remote tools so you can regulate your spend with us to ensure that even when a PBX is compromised, you remain in control.

We also provide Ethernet over Fibre Connectivity to your remote sites, with Internet Connectivity through our network. Whilst it is natural to deploy your own firewalls, we apply our learning here too - filtering the worst VoIP hackers from ever reaching your perimeter. We can also provide an unfiltered list of identified bad IP addresses in real-time. The result is a simple way to prevent loss of income through malicious use of your telephony network.

[1]To request a copy of VoIP Fraud Analysis please visit the link in the appendix.

Chapter 2

THE INTEGRITY
OF CALLER ID

When you receive a phone call on your mobile, or a desk phone capable of displaying a number, you may be inclined to trust the Caller ID that is shown. Fraudsters and scam marketers rely on this. If the person answering has an expectation of where the caller is from, or who the caller is, any deception is so much easier. It plays directly to the human tendency towards confirmation bias and susceptibility to pre-conditioning.

I n the old days, when a phone was simply connected to the telephone network by a piece of wire, all caller IDs were set by the network and there were relatively few networks. Nowadays, caller IDs – one that is visible to the core recipient and others that are hidden and for network use only – can be set by the calling device. The role of the service provider is to ensure that these are correct, to override them when appropriate, and to police that they have been set in the first place. At carrier level, there is an implied level of trust that other carriers and their service providers have done this. At Simwood we go to some considerable lengths to ensure we are only passing valid and relevant caller ID. Sadly, again, we find ourselves in the minority.

Therefore, it is relatively easy for a fraudster or a scam marketer to sign up for a telephone service online, and to be passing calls with their own choice of caller ID, or no caller ID at all, in a matter of moments.

If your systems, your processes or your people rely on caller ID in any way, and presume it to be authoritative, this can be a potential security threat to your business. The fundamental message here is that caller ID cannot and should not be trusted.

Beyond the human-engineering vulnerabilities, keep in mind other devices that sometimes rely on caller ID. Think of door locks or security alarms that open/disarm on receipt of a call from a known

"If your systems, your processes, or your people, rely on caller ID in any way, and presume it to be authoritative, this can be a potential security threat to your business. The caller ID cannot and should not be trusted"

number. Some companies also allow authorised CLIs to dial into their corporate PBX, creating an open door for VoIP Fraud or other deception.

Of course, this cuts both ways. Whilst you should not trust caller ID on calls you receive, it is just as easy for a scammer to make outbound calls representing one of *your* numbers as the point of origin. As a wholesale service provider with millions of numbers allocated to us by Ofcom, this has been a particular problem for us over the years. Since Ofcom mandated that marketing callers could not withhold their caller ID, scam marketers have taken to presenting a random local number on calls they are making to a particular area. Thankfully, in most cases these numbers are unallocated and thus there is no victim business wrongly accused of the crime. However, it is simple to identify the service provider to whom that number is allocated. As a result, we have found ourselves the recipients of understandable public frustration for nuisance calls that we have neither made nor transited, but that have been made presenting one of our unallocated numbers as the origin.

If someone were to return a call to these numbers they would be routed to the operator who actually controlled that number, or the end-user to whom it is routed. However, the call presenting that number as a

caller ID can occur without the operator of authority – or indeed the end-user business to which that number is allocated – being in any way involved.

Caller ID spoofing, whilst very trivial to effect, represents a threat to your business both in terms of inbound calls with a wrong number presented, or outbound calls where reputational damage or fraud in your name are entirely possible.

Whilst we cannot prevent a rogue operative placing calls purporting to come from your numbers, if your actual numbers were on the Simwood network, we'd be on the front-line for any complaints and investigations. As the operator that has always tried to educate customers on the risks (even when regulators and operators were denying it was possible), Simwood is active in mitigating caller ID fraud.

For calls coming into your organisation, we have a number of algorithms that can help screen nuisance/fraudulent calls. Because we connect into other operators like BT over SS7, we see far more information about a call than those (surprisingly large and numerous) operators that resell BT's IP service. We understand and apply this extra data for our Intelligent Caller Reject feature (available for any or all incoming numbers) and have developed bespoke solutions for the particular challenges faced by individual sectors – for example, Financial Services.

If you face any of the challenges mentioned in this chapter then we would welcome the opportunity to discuss them in detail and explore together how Simwood can help.

Chapter 3

....

"ENCRYPTION IS POINTLESS"

I was enraged to read this comment, made by the CEO of a large UK service provider on an industry mailing list. Sadly, his point is not an outlier or unique to him. It also highlights the difference in stance that Simwood takes relative to the rest of the industry. The reality is that if you are passing telephone calls today they are highly likely to be unencrypted and easy to intercept.

I n past times, when services were delivered over a piece of wire to your building and phones connected at the end, call intercept was always possible. However, it required a trained engineer, somewhere in the physical path of the call – probably at the green box down the street – who was able to identify the particular pair of wires that your call was carried over so they could connect listening probes. Agencies that had a need could work with the service provider to intercept calls deeper in the network as well. Even so, casual intercept was relatively difficult and there was a presumed level of privacy to a moderate standard.

In today's multinational business world you may be speaking to suppliers or lawyers on different continents. Or you may have homeworkers linking in over domestic connections. Or travelling workers making calls over hotel Wi-Fi. In short, the landscape has changed dramatically. With VoIP, the voice is only as secure as the IP. A call made on hotel or coffee shop Wi-Fi that is unencrypted, even domestic broadband, are all open to casual intercept by anybody else on that network. Beyond the access network, the calls traverse a service provider, often several service providers, before eventually reaching the VoIP reseller, who often passes it on to another reseller, who passes it on to

"The fewer hops along the way, the fewer opportunities to break the encryption that you have enabled"

another reseller, and so on. At the ultimate carrier, calls will be transited to another carrier and then the reverse hierarchy is followed until the call arrives at its destination. The more VoIP extends to end users, and the more nomadic those end users are, the more important encryption becomes because there are so many more opportunities for casual or targeted snooping to take place.

But that's okay, because IP protocols (and VoIP is no exception) have encryption and privacy baked into their specification, right? Sadly, that specification requires implementation. And whilst a

user would not contemplate connecting to a banking website that did not display the trusty encryption padlock in a browser, no such security expectation is made with regard to telephone calls. By default most VoIP software defaults to unencrypted audio over unencrypted transport. Therefore, it is no surprise that most service providers, and much of their hierarchy of less technically adept resellers, do not enable it. We know from our own experience servicing hundreds of service providers, and offering encryption as a promoted feature of our carrier services, that the majority do not care. The quote in the title captures this perfectly.

At the very least, if you are deploying a VoIP PBX (as you probably already have done), you should ensure that encryption is enabled at all of your endpoints. In particular, those that are nomadic. You should also make sure you encrypt any service provider connection out from your PBX, and question their own infrastructure. If they have any, that is. Unfortunately, we operate in a world where it seems many "resellers" claim to be a "carrier" and the truth is often difficult to find. Yet the key point here is that your business-critical calls should not be carried unencrypted across yet another third party's infrastructure, or the public Internet.

Whilst I agree with nothing in the quote given in the title, there is one slightly defensible aspect to it. That is the fact that VoIP encryption, rather like your connection to a banking website, is point-to-point. The core difference here though is that when you connect your banking website the website is one point, and your browser is the other point. Thus point-to-point encryption is entirely feasible because it serves simply to protect the contents in transit from

any snooping between those points. In the VoIP world, there are many points in a given call. A call will originate with a desk or soft-phone and transit an IP network to another point which is your corporate PBX. From your corporate PBX, it will transit an IP network to your service provider's PBX or proxy. Then it will cross the next service provider's PBX or proxy, to their service provider's proxy. All of this before moving on to the carrier's proxy, the next carrier's proxy and so on. Encryption should be enabled between each pair of these points along the way. But it probably won't be. Even if it is, any other pair of points that are unencrypted still pose an intercept threat. Yet the fact remains that the greatest risk of targeted or casual snooping on your phone calls is at either end of the call. We continue to implore other service providers to enable encryption, but it is incumbent upon you as the customer to ensure that encryption is present from your own end points and that your service provider is able to support it. Whilst standards for end-to-end encryption exist, the most practical solution for minimising intercept opportunities you have at the moment, is to ensure that your supply chain is as short as possible (i.e. deal with a carrier, not a reseller). The fewer hops along the way, the fewer opportunities to break the encryption that you have enabled.

"We operate in a world where it seems many 'resellers' claim to be a 'carrier' and the truth is often difficult to find"

When it comes to your choice of carrier it is worth noting that big is not always beautiful. VoIP is a very technical discipline, and there are very few experts in the field. The big carrier approach to VoIP tends to be to purchase a 'magic box' and to pay a consultancy to have it installed. This approach is very different to that taken by the likes of Simwood. We are a core part of the communities that actually write the open source software, and we understand and develop our own technologies. By way of example, the incumbent operator has services that compete with ours – in offering IP telephony services to service providers. We support encryption yet they do not. So whilst encryption is optional for our service provider customers, it is at least possible. For the incumbents' resellers and their end users in turn, it is not.

We have always championed encryption in our industry. And, while we are pleased that others show signs of catching up, customers know that it is available today on Simwood and has been since 2010. Whether for PCI or simple privacy, all your inbound and outbound calls can be encrypted between your equipment and ours. There is no additional feature charge for this! And because Simwood is the carrier, your calls are (by definition) encrypted all the way to the PSTN. There is no hierarchy of resellers in between who will pass call legs around unencrypted. Switching your VoIP calls (in and out) to Simwood will give you this peace of mind straightaway.

Chapter 4

AND DON'T THINK MOBILE IS SAFE

By this stage, you might be thinking that VoIP is unsafe and should be avoided. You might even think of following what seems to have become a corporate trend of preferring mobile devices over desk phones because they are more secure. This is not the case.

VoIP has all of the necessary features and security attributes within its open specification to be secure. It simply requires the implementer to understand them, to enable them, and for the supply chain to support them. We maintain that the Simwood service, or that of one of our more proactive customers, will be far more secure than any other voice communications service available.

To the point about mobile, the SIM card in your mobile device carries cryptographic keys, known only to the network that issued your SIM card. However, there are two things you have to understand:

1 Those cryptographic keys exist to enable encryption over the air (i.e. the radio leg to the mast), to prevent casual interception. From that point on, the call is likely to be unencrypted. It is also worth noting that most operators use well-known cryptographic algorithms, which may be susceptible to compromise.

2 Encryption can be turned off on 2G.

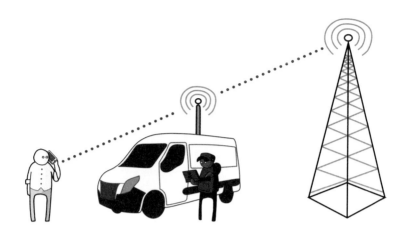

The second bullet point is probably the most significant here. You may think that 2G died out long ago and that because you have 3G or 4G coverage then mandatory encryption applies, at least over the air. This is not necessarily the case.

"One of the most common 'front-end' attack vectors is to deploy a dummy cell, which encourages target devices to join on 2G – then turns off the encryption!"

˝ One of the most common 'front-end' attack vectors is to deploy a dummy cell ('IMSI Grabber' or 'Stingray'), which encourages target devices to join on 2G - then turns off the encryption! Phones will appear to work as normal, albeit with only 2G service, but all calls and SMS will be proxied through a 'man in the middle'. We have first-hand experience of how this is used for good, but we have also experienced it used for bad. I spoke at a telephony conference at which there were two IMSI grabbers active in the room. They were only identified due to their interference with the radio microphones.

In many parts of the world, 2G remains the standard. Travelling employees phoning home, or speaking to customers, are potentially exposed to state intercept or the less obvious use of IMSI grabbers.

Beyond this over-the-air vulnerability, there is an increasing tendency for mobile networks to supply businesses and home users with femtocells, which connect into the corporate or home IP network. There is no way of assuring what level of security is present on these or their own vulnerability to external intrusions and control. One major UK operator is said to have suffered a breach of its femtocells in 2011, enabling hackers to turn them into IMSI grabbers[2].

An over-the-top VoIP application to a competent service provider, with encryption fully enabled, offers a far more secure means of communication for your business than a routine commodity mobile service. The gold standard though is a proper VoLTE (Voice over LTE/4G) service with a security architecture built by people who know what they're doing, and care.

imwood does not yet have a solution here as it would require securing third party devices on third party networks. We know what a Simwood solution would look like though and the next chapter highlights some of the building blocks we are putting in place.

[2]To read more about this significant hack, see article link in the appendix.

Chapter 5

HACKING YOUR
MOBILE FROM
THE OTHER SIDE
OF THE WORLD

If I told you that it was possible – with no knowledge on your part or interruption to your service – for somebody to intercept your mobile calls and text messages from the other side of the world, you might think I was being far-fetched. Yet this is entirely possible and increasingly used by security agencies and abused by fraudsters.

Mobile devices, unlike their fixed-line counterparts or nomadic VoIP users, need to be able to travel the world and utilise the radio spectrum and network of overseas mobile operators. Mobile operators are therefore all interconnected with the capability existing for one provider to query another provider's network. They can interrogate such things as handset location and pose queries to the network, such as whether to allow a user to connect.

"This is a problem that we at Simwood are devoting significant resources to solving"

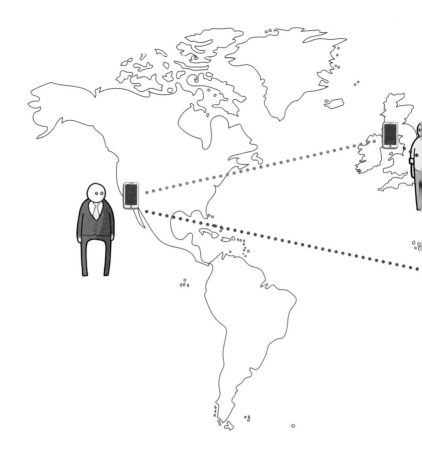

The signalling technology that is used by Mobile Network Operators (MNOs) to control mobile telephones – the SS7 network – is far from open. However, it is certainly not closed. A hacker with access to it, perhaps by virtue of their employment or having been established as a mobile operator for this purpose, can trivially interrogate the status of your mobile phone. By doing so, they can discern such things as what country you are in and whether you are online. Less trivially, they can update this status in order to reroute your voice calls and SMS messages. This allows them to create a 'man in the middle' situation where all calls and SMS to and from your mobile device are transited through a monitoring station in clear text. Not only does this form of 'back-end' attack pose a security threat when your employees use their mobile phones to communicate with customers, suppliers, or indeed corporate HQ. It also poses a significant threat to other security protocols you have that rely upon these mechanisms.

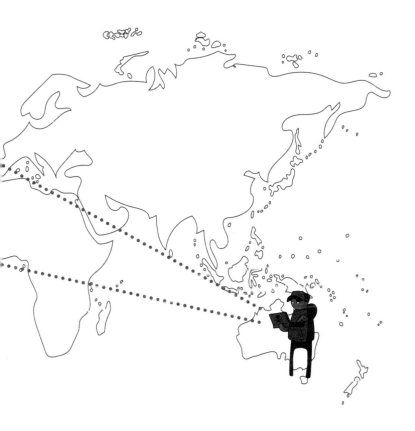

"For around $250, anyone can buy an interception service that will collect the voice and SMS of just about any mobile phone on the planet"

This is a problem that we at Simwood are devoting significant resources to solving. Back-end attacks can be detected and stopped with multi-layered security strategies.

One example of how back-end attacks can compromise other security systems is the use of SMS as a part of a two-factor authentication mechanism. Users are sent one-time passwords or "Was this payment made by you?" type SMS messages to their mobile device as a way of authenticating some other transaction, usually made online. This mechanism is perfectly acceptable if the endpoint is secure, but it poses a significant threat if it is not.

You may think that this is a high tech and thus high stakes intrusion vector that is unlikely to be used in low level financial fraud. But that is exactly the place that it is being used, and it is commonly available as a commodity service on the 'Dark Web'. For around $250, anyone can buy an interception service that will collect the voice and SMS of just about any mobile phone on the planet, subject to protections that the mobile phone operator may have put in place. Having successfully phished a victim, and identified from their compromised email whom they bank with and their mobile number, it is a matter of cost versus reward for a fraudster to contract to intercept their SMS. Armed with this information, they will be able to intercept and respond to any one-time passwords or other authentication using SMS.

For this purpose, SMS is currently the most ubiquitous and well-understood means of communication with end users that enterprises have. However, it should be used with awareness of the risks. There is no solution on the market known to us. As previously mentioned, Simwood is working hard to develop one. Once complete, the sender of an SMS will be able to identify the sovereignty of the endpoint, and gauge the likelihood that an intercept has taken place.

At the time of writing Simwood is actively building and acquiring the necessary assets to be a full mobile network operator, complementing our existing assets in the ordinary fixed-line world. This means that rather than using someone else's SS7 access (as agencies and rogue operatives would) we will be an MNO in our own right with privileged access to other MNO networks. Our reasoning is to build solutions for our Financial Services customers and enable them to tackle the threats identified in this guide.

These solutions will be presented either as a restricted API interface that can ask "Is this mobile intercepted?" type questions, or baked into our two-way SMS and voice-call services. In other words, we are building up to a position where we can certify whether the device you are calling, texting or are being contacted from has been compromised.

If this is an issue that is relevant to your business, we would welcome your support in developing an enterprise-ready solution.

Chapter 6

IT'S STILL ABOUT THE HUMANS

Many of the attack vectors identified in this document have been 'high tech', and require some level of engineering ability. Yet not all crime involving telecoms networks has to involve a high level of technical involvement. Human Engineering techniques are still widely used to gain access to communications systems, and often present the easiest option.

One example of a Human Engineering attack is a SIM-swap. In this vector, a fraudster who has already identified his or her victim is likely to have used a phishing attack to gain access to bank account details, mobile phone and other personal details (such as date of birth, National Insurance number, home address). They then use this collateral to trick the victim's mobile operator into reissuing the SIM card - the means of gaining network access. The most common way of doing this is for the fraudster to go into a mobile phone shop, claim to be the target user and say they have lost their phone and SIM. After satisfying the shop staff that they are the target user, the shop will issue a replacement SIM that then takes on the identity of the 'lost' SIM.

On inserting that SIM card into the fraudster's phone, they will be able to carry out their fraud and receive any phone calls or SMS intended for the victim. At this stage, our victim remains unaware of the scam, except for a possible loss of service. Combined with other information they already have, such as bank account logins, our fraudster is now in a position to receive one-time codes via SMS that are intended to be the second check of the victim's identity.

"A fraudster who has already identified his or her victim, probably through a phishing attack, can trick the victim's mobile operator into reissuing the SIM card - the means of gaining network access"

CONCLUSION

Your colleagues' awareness and responsiveness to threats are an issue way beyond the solutions touched upon in this guide. However, technology can help. With specific reference to SIM-swap, Simwood is actively building technology that can identify compromised mobile devices (see Chapter 5) for key existing clients.

In the interim, using Simwood for your call termination means we are in a position to help. For example, we can detect whether a call to a mobile phone has been forwarded elsewhere – an indicator of compromise – as well as where the device is.

Furthermore, the solutions presented earlier can identify whether an incoming call purporting to be from your customer is legitimate or has been spoofed.

Every business has its own unique telephony challenges. We would love to help you tackle yours

Our business is telecoms. So we certainly hope we have not persuaded you that telecoms are to be avoided! Even if we had, the reality is that your business could not exist without them. Our aim is to educate and inform, in the hope that you will become aware of existing threats to your business beyond those found in the brochures of 'magic box' vendors.

We punch well above our weight in international circles thanks to our engineering skills. We make it our business to identify and mitigate the threats that you have read about in this guide. And we do our best to bang the drum within our own industry in the hope that others will start to care more about their customers' security.

Our experience tells us that we have a lot more work to do. We remain deeply concerned at the effect this is having on end users of telecommunication services. Writing this guide is a fairly unprecedented step in sharing with executives of major UK enterprises the level of risk they are exposed to by their current service provision.

If you have found this guide useful, do please let us know. In fact, we welcome your feedback in any form.

APPENDIX

Further Reading:

[1]To request a copy of VoIP Fraud Analysis please visit
https://simwood.com/voipfraudanalysis17

[2]'Vodafone femtocell hack lets intruders listen to
calls' ZDNet, 14 July 2011
http://www.zdnet.com/article/vodafone-femtocell-
hack-lets-intruders-listen-to-calls/

Chapter 1 - 'Your whole network as a SIP IPS'
Kamailio World 2016, 20 May 2016
http://blog.simwood.com/2016/05/kamailio-world-
fraud-talks/

Chapter 1 - 'Simwood's VoIP Fraud Analysis'
ClueCon Weekly, 3 February 2016
http://blog.simwood.com/2016/02/cluecon-weekly-
call/

Chapter 3 - 'Encryption is Pointless' Simwood Blog,
26 June 2017
http://blog.simwood.com/2017/06/encryption-is-
pointless/

Chapter 5 - 'NSA intercepts Angela Merkel's
private phone' CNN, 4 July 2015
http://edition.cnn.com/2015/07/03/politics/
germany-media-spying-obama-administration/

Chapter 5 - 'Putin knows how easy it is to hack
mobile phones, he doesn't use them' TIME, 24
March 2014
http://time.com/35932/ukraine-russia-putin-
spies-kgb/

Chapter 5 - 'SS7 vulnerability and just how easy
it is to hack into calls from across the world' 60
Minutes, 19 April 2016
https://www.youtube.com/
watch?v=O4tUx1W3zLc&feature=youtu.be

Chapter 5 - 'How the NSA hack phone networks'
The Intercept, 4 December 2014
https://theintercept.com/2014/12/04/nsa-
auroragold-hack-cellphones/

Chapter 6 - 'SIM Swap through your bank is a
legitimate threat' Aspect, 27 July 2017
https://www.aspect.com/uk/company/news-
and-events/press-releases/uk-press-releases/
emerging-mobile-technology-can-tackle-ongoing-
issue-of-social-engineering-fraud

For convenience, all are available via simwood.com/SecurityBook

INTRODUCING
SIMWOOD

We believe the convergence of telecoms technologies can change the world for the better and we exist to enable that change. From developer-friendly APIs and human-friendly interfaces to our unconventional approach to fraud protection, we empower our customers and champion a fair and transparent telecoms marketplace.

We have spent over 20 years ensuring we own, or at least control, every element of the infrastructure underpinning our service. That way we give businesses that share our outlook the best service levels and fastest access to new technology possible. Together we will out-innovate and out-deliver 'me too' providers and give your end users what they deserve: secure and stable telephony they can trust.